CW01390898

This book belongs to:

_____

_____

A Treasury for
Three
Year Olds

A Treasury for Three Year Olds

A Collection of Stories,
Fairy Tales and Nursery Rhymes

p

Language Consultant: Betty Root.

This is a Parragon book
This edition published in 2006

Parragon
Queen Street House
4 Queen Street
Bath BA1 1HE, UK

Copyright © Parragon Books Ltd 2001

All rights reserved. No part of this publication may
be reproduced, stored in a retrieval system, or transmitted by
any means, electronic, mechanical, photocopying, recording,
or otherwise, without the prior permission of the copyright
holder.

Printed in China

1-40546-932-3

✦ Contents ✦

9

The Ugly Duckling

It was a beautiful summer's day. The sun shone brightly on Mother Duck as she lay her eggs. "Quack, quack," she went, as she stood up to count the eggs. "Gosh, that egg is a really big one," she thought. "It will probably turn out to be a big strong drake, like Father Duck." Happy, she settled back down on her nest.

Mother Duck had been sitting on her eggs for a long time when, suddenly,

CR . . . ACK

CR . . . ACK, the eggs began to hatch. One by one, the yellow ducklings appeared. Soon, Mother Duck had four beautiful fluffy babies. Now only the really big egg was left.

Mother Duck sat patiently on the really big egg until, at last, CR . . . ACK, out burst a duckling. But my, what an ugly duckling it was! It was large and grey, and not at all beautiful like the others. "Hmmm," thought Mother Duck, "perhaps it isn't a duckling after all. I'll take it to the water and see."

"Follow me," called Mother Duck. One, two, three, four, five . . . the ducklings hurried after her. SPLASH! She jumped into the river. "Quack, quack!" she called out, and all the ducklings splashed into the water. Soon all of them, even the ugly grey one, were swimming along.

Next, Mother Duck introduced her babies to the other ducks around the farmyard. "Now, my dears," she said quietly, "bow your heads and say 'quack' to the Old Duck."

All the ducklings, even the ugly grey one, did as they were told. But the other ducks just laughed when they saw the ugly duckling.

"I've never seen anything so ugly," said one.

"What is that?" asked another.

"Come here," called the Old Duck to Mother Duck. "Let me see your children. Hmm! All are very pretty, except that big one."

"He might be ugly," said Mother Duck, "but he swims well."

"Such a pity!" sighed the Old Duck.

Life around the farmyard was very happy for the four yellow ducklings. But the ugly duckling had a terrible time. He was very unhappy. All the ducks and hens teased him because he was so ugly, and no one ever let him join in the fun.

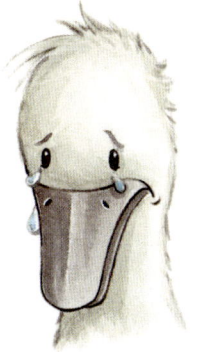

One day, the ugly duckling decided to run away. He scrambled down to the river and began to swim as fast as he could – away from the farmyard, away from Mother Duck and away from the four beautiful yellow ducklings. Soon he met two wild geese. "You are ugly," laughed the geese. "You are really so ugly that we cannot help but like you. Won't you come and fly with us?"

But the ugly ducking couldn't leave with them because he didn't know how to fly.

Cluck, cluck!

Hiss, hiss!

He walked on and on, until he came to a hut. Inside the hut lived an old woman, a cat and a hen.

"Hiss, hiss!" went the cat.

"Cluck, cluck!" went the hen.

"What, what?" went the old woman. "Look's like we'll be eating duck's eggs from now on."

And so the ugly duckling was allowed to stay. Of course, no eggs appeared. The hen and the cat teased the duckling.

"Can you lay eggs, like me?" asked the hen.

"No," replied the duckling.

"Can you purr, like me?" asked the cat.

"No," replied the duckling.

"Quite ugly! Quite useless!" went the cat and the hen together.

The ugly duckling wandered back to the river where he spent his days alone. Soon, winter came and the weather became icy. The duckling grew tired and cold. One day a farmer rescued the ugly duckling and carried him home. The farmer's children tried to play with him but, thinking they were teasing him, he jumped into the milk pail. Milk spilled everywhere

"AHHH!"

"Ahhhh!" screamed the farmer's wife.

"Ha! Ha!" laughed the farmer's children.

Luckily the door was open, and the duckling flew out.

The ugly duckling was happy when spring arrived at last. He flapped his wings and soared into the sky. Below, he saw a garden with a large lake in the middle. On the lake were some beautiful white swans.

"I must go down to them," thought the ugly duckling.

He landed on the water and swam towards the swans. They raced forwards to meet him. The duckling bent his head, expecting to be attacked. Instead, he saw

his own reflection in
the water. He could
hardly believe his eyes.
He was no longer an ugly
grey duckling. He was a beautiful white swan.

As the other swans fussed around their new friend,
some children came to the water's edge. "Look,
there's a new swan on the lake," cried one. "It's the
most beautiful swan I've ever seen." Then the old
swans bowed before the young swan. He had never
been so happy in his whole life!

Hey, Diddle, Diddle

Hey, diddle, diddle,
The cat and the fiddle,
The cow jumped over the moon;
The little dog laughed to see such sport,
And the dish ran away with the spoon.

Five Little Ducks

Five little ducks went swimming one day,
Over the pond and far away.
Mother Duck went "Quack, quack, quack".
But only four little ducks came back.

Four little ducks went swimming one day,
Over the pond and far away.
Mother Duck went "Quack, quack, quack".
But only three little ducks came back.

Three little ducks went swimming one day,
Over the pond and far away.
Mother Duck went "Quack, quack, quack".
But only two little ducks came back.

Two little ducks went swimming one day,
Over the pond and far away.
Mother Duck went "Quack, quack, quack".
But only one little duck came back.

One little duck went swimming one day,
Over the pond and far away.
Mother Duck went "Quack, quack, quack".
And five little ducks came swimming back.

We Won't Budge!

It was a hot, hot day in a hot, hot country. The watering-holes were definitely the coolest place to be. But there had been no rain for days, so there was just enough water for one group of animals at a time to stand in the watering-hole. The animals decided to take turns. Today it was the turn of the hippos, and one thing was for sure . . . the hippos were definitely not going to budge.

"We're cool," they gloated noisily to the other animals.

"Pleeeeese!" whined the sweating vultures near the edge of the water. "Pleeeeese could we have an incy-wincy turn?"

But the hippos just chanted: "We won't budge!" So the vultures tap-tap-tapped on the hippos' hard skin with their sharp beaks to teach them a lesson. But hippos are thick skinned in more ways than one, and they didn't feel a thing.

"Pleasssssssse!" hissed the snakes, slithering near the edge of the water. "Pleasssssssse could we have a slithery slice of a turn?"

But the hippos just chanted: "We won't budge!"

"We won't budge!"

So the snakes coiled their long bodies tightly round the hippos' legs and tried to pull them out! But hippos are strong in

more ways than one, and they won't ever move unless they want to.

"Plehee-hee-ease!" neighed the zebras, hoping for a tiny share of the water. "Plehee-hee-ease could we have the thinnest stripe of a turn?"

But the hippos just chanted: "We won't budge!"
So the zebras all pawed at the ground with their hooves, trying to scare the hippos away. But hippos are brave in more ways than one, and they didn't even blink an eyelid. And one thing was for sure . . . and they said it again, "WE WON'T BUDGE!"

"WE WON'T BUDGE!"

As the sun grew hotter, more and more animals came to the watering-hole. They stood around its edge, staring across at the selfish hippos. But the hippos weren't going to budge even for the gentle antelopes, who helped them out by swatting flies from their ears with their swishing tails. Today, those cool hippos standing in the cool water of the watering-hole were not going to budge – for anyone!

Suddenly there came a noise that made the hippos look up. Every ear of every hippo twitched, and listened. It was a noise that made the antelopes and zebras and snakes and vultures sprint and gallop and slither and fly away in an instant.

DER-UM! DER-UM! DR-UM! DR-UM!

DRM! DRM! DRM!

The hippos stood up. Their eyes grew wider, and their great strong legs trembled. Their hard skins shivered, and they didn't know what to do.

DER-UM! DER-UM! DER-UM!
DER-UM!

"Help!" whispered the littlest hippo very quietly.

"We won't budge," whispered the biggest hippo even more quietly.

There was silence, except for the thundering dust-cloud approaching the watering-hole.

"WE WILL BUDGE!" exclaimed all the hippos together, as they rushed away.

The thundering dust was in fact an enomous herd of heavy elephants. They were thirsty and hot, and they weren't going to be put off cooling their feet. So the elephants carried on running towards the watering-hole until they splashed right into the middle of the pool.

"Aaaaah!" sighed the elephants, trumpeting their happiness. And all the other animals (except those brave old hippos) sneaked back to take a look at them.

"One thing is definitely for sure," called the sweating vultures. "Those cool elephants are not going to budge for anyone."

But it didn't matter, because the elephants saw how hot and bothered the vultures and the snakes and the antelopes were under the scorching sun. They counted: "One and . . . two and . . . three and . . .". Then they sucked up the water into their long bendy trunks, pointed, squinted, aimed and fired the water at the animals all around.

"Aaaah!"
"Aaaah!" sighed the antelopes.
"Aaaah!" neighed the zebras.
"Aaaah!" hissed the snakes.
"Aaaah!" croaked the vultures.

27

"Aaaaaaah!" sighed the hippos, who were standing a long way off watching everything. If only they could be sprayed too. And slowly, very slowly, hardly knowing what they were doing, the hot hippos made their way back to the watering-hole.

But there was only room for one group of animals at a time to stand in the water. Now it was the elephants' turn. And one thing was for sure . . . "WE WON'T BUDGE!" they called out, when they saw the hippos approaching.

"Pleeeeeeeeeease!" pleaded the hippos. "Plehee-hee-ease could we have the chunkiest chunk of a turn?"

"No you can't!" trumped the cool elephants. "That's just greedy."

"Hurrah!" cheered the antelopes, the snakes, the zebras and the vultures. They all remembered very well that the hippos didn't budge for them – or squirt them.

28

So the hot hippos, with their burning hot skins, tramped away from the watering-hole. And the elephants watched them go, and felt very sorry for them. They counted: "One and . . . two and . . . three and . . .". Then they sucked up the water into their long bendy trunks, pointed, squinted, aimed and fired at the hippos.

"ONE! TWO! THREE!"

"Aaaaaaaaaaaaaaaah!" sighed the hippos.

And one thing was for sure . . . they were definitely NOT going to budge.

"Aaaaaaah!"

Round and Round
the Garden

Round and round the garden,
Like a teddy bear.

One step,
Two steps,
Tickle you under there!

This Little Piggy

This little piggy went to market,
This little piggy stayed at home,
This little piggy had roast beef,
And this little piggy had none,
And this little piggy cried,
"Wee-wee-wee-wee-wee"
All the way home.

Incy Wincy Spider

Incy Wincy Spider,
Climbing up the spout;
Down came the rain,
And washed the spider out;
Out came the sun,
And dried up all the rain;
So Incy Wincy Spider
Climbed up the spout again.

Cuthbert, the Lonely Crocodile

Cuthbert the crocodile is lonely. All the other animals in the jungle seem to have lots of brothers and sisters, or lots of friends. They play together all day long, laughing and chasing each other, climbing trees and running beside the water.

Cuthbert watches them and sighs. No one notices him or asks if he would like to play too. At last, Cuthbert asks his mother if he can have a baby brother to play with.

"Oh dear, Cuthbert," she says. "I am too busy looking after all my eggs to think about anything else at the moment. Run along now! And please stop looking so miserable! It is a lovely sunny day. You should be smiling and happy."

32

"Hey! Mind that tail of yours!" calls his mother. "It very nearly knocked all my eggs down the bank just now."

Cuthbert sets off for a walk along the river bank. After a while, he sees Lara Leopard snoozing in the warm sunshine.

"Please, Lara," asks Cuthbert, "do you think one of your little cub brothers will be my baby brother, too?"

"No!" says Lara Leopard. "They are too frightened of your teeth to play with you. And anyway, Mother is washing their ears right now."

Next, Cuthbert calls up to Mrs Parrot who is chattering in the trees:

"Hello, Mrs Parrot. You have a lot of chicks in your nest. Can you

spare one of them to play with me, please?"

"No, no, no," says Mrs Parrot. "My little chicks are far too small to leave the nest – far too small, far too small! I'm sure they'll play with you once their feathers have grown and they can fly. But today they are too tiny – far too tiny, far too tiny!"

So Cuthbert waddles off along the river bank to see if Erma Elephant will lend him her little son.

"Oh no!" says Erma. "My darling son is my only child, and I could not bear to part with him. I'm sure he will play with you soon, but today he is having a bath. Then he has to learn how to squirt water."

Next, Cuthbert calls up to Clare Chimpanzee who is peering at him through the leaves.

"Please, Clare, please could you spare one of your twin babies to come down here and play with me?"

"No, I'm sorry," replies Clare Chimpanzee. "My babies like it up here, swinging through the trees and riding on my back. They would be very, very unhappy in your damp swamp. Sorry, Cuthbert! But don't look so sad. I'm sure you'll soon find a friend who wants to play."

Cuthbert continues to the edge of the jungle, and then heads out towards the mountains, to the cave where the gorillas live.

"Hello!" he calls. "Hello, little gorillas! Please will you play with me?"

To Cuthbert's surprise, two gorilla babies come running out of the cave. They are very pleased to see him. The cubs start to play with Cuthbert for a while, rolling down the mountainside, laughing and giggling – but then Mother Gorilla calls them back inside.

"Hurry up! It's time for your supper," she says. "Stop playing with Cuthbert and come back into the cave."

"... Supper!"

"Goodbye!" call the two gorilla babies. "Come and play again soon, Cuthbert!"

So now Cuthbert is alone again. He walks slowly back home. He waves to the chimpanzees and the elephants. He waves to the leopards. It is getting late. Bright eyes peep at Cuthbert from the dark shadows as he scurries along the path. At last he reaches the riverbank.

"Quick!" croak the frogs. "Hurry up, Cuthbert! Your mother has a wonderful surprise waiting for you."

Cuthbert rushes up the slippery bank to the top where his mother is waiting and smiling.

"Look!" grunts his mother proudly. "Look Cuthbert, my eggs have hatched."

Cuthbert stares in amazement. He cannot believe his eyes. In front of him are ten baby crocodiles. He crouches down to take a closer look. The babies climb up onto Cuthbert and stare at him.

"Hello, Cuthbert," squeak ten little crocodile voices. In an instant the ten little babies are swarming all over Cuthbert, sitting on his head, sliding down his nose and swinging on his long tail.

"They're tickling me!" he laughs, as his mother watches them carefully – to make sure the little creatures do not fall off Cuthbert's nose or slip down the riverbank.

"You are our very own big brother," squeaks one baby crocodile.

"Will you play with us?" squeaks another.

37

"Yes! Please! Do play with us!" they all squeak together.

Cuthbert's happy face grins as only a crocodile face can. At last he has brothers and sisters to play with. In fact, he has more brothers and sisters than anyone else in the jungle!

Old MacDonald Had a Farm

Old MacDonald had a farm,
ee-i-ee-i-o!
And on that farm he had some cows,
ee-i-ee-i-o!
With a moo-moo here,
And a moo-moo there,
Here a moo, there a moo, everywhere
a moo-moo,
Old MacDonald had a farm,
ee-i-ee-i-o!

Old MacDonald had a farm,
ee-i-ee-i-o!
And on that farm he had some sheep,
ee-i-ee-i-o!
With a baa-baa here,
And a baa-baa there,
Here a baa, there a baa, everywhere
a baa-baa,
Old MacDonald had a farm,
ee-i-ee-i-o!

Old MacDonald had a farm,
ee-i-ee-i-o!
And on that farm he had some horses,
ee-i-ee-i-o!
With a neigh-neigh here,
And a neigh-neigh there,
Here a neigh, there a neigh, everywhere a
neigh-neigh,
Old MacDonald had a farm,
ee-i-ee-i-o!

Old MacDonald had a farm,
ee-i-ee-i-o!
And on that farm he had some pigs,
ee-i-ee-i-o!
With an oink-oink here,
And an oink-oink there,
Here an oink, there an oink,
everywhere an oink-oink,
Old MacDonald had a farm,
ee-i-ee-i-o!

Old MacDonald had a farm,
ee-i-ee-i-o!
And on that farm he had some ducks,
ee-i-ee-i-o!
With a quack-quack here,
And a quack-quack there,
Here a quack, there a quack,
everywhere a quack-quack,
Old MacDonald had a farm,
ee-i-ee-i-o!

The Princess and the Pea

Once upon a time, in a faraway place, there lived a handsome prince. Now this prince wanted to get married. But he didn't want to marry an ordinary girl. He wanted to marry a real princess.

The prince travelled from place to place in search of a wife. But the prince didn't know how to tell the difference between a real princess and a pretend one. He found lots of princesses but there was always something wrong with them.

Some were too tall. Some were too small. Some were too silly. Some were too serious. There was even one that was too pretty!

After the prince had travelled far and wide, he began to think he would never ever find a real princess, and so he returned home. The prince became more and more unhappy. His father and mother, the king and queen, were very worried. They did not know what to do about their sad son.

Then one dark, stormy night there was a knock at the palace door. The old king himself went to open the door. You can imagine how surprised he was to find a soaking-wet girl shivering before him.

"Come in, come in," said the kind king. "Who are you? Why are you outdoors on such a terrible night?"

43

"Hello, I'm a princess," the girl told the surprised king. "I'm afraid I became quite lost in the storm. Please can I sleep here for the night?"

The king stared at the girl in disbelief. But the prince began to smile when he heard her musical voice and saw her beautiful smile. The queen looked carefully at the girl's dripping-wet clothes and wild straggly hair.

"Ah, we shall soon see whether you're a real princess or not," she thought. "There's one sure way of finding out." However, the queen did not tell anyone about her plan.

Quietly, the queen tiptoed into the guest bedroom. She took all the sheets and blankets off the bed and put three tiny peas on top of the mattress. Then she placed twenty more mattresses, one on top of the other,

over the peas. Finally, she put twenty feather quilts on top of the mattresses. The bed was so high that the poor princess needed a ladder to climb onto it.

The next morning, the queen asked the princess how she had slept.

"I hardly slept a wink last night," replied the princess.

"I had a terrible night. There was something very hard in my bed. I'm bruised all over."

Now it was obvious to the queen that only a real princess could feel three tiny peas through twenty mattresses and twenty feather quilts. Everyone agreed that she was indeed a real princess.

The prince was so happy to find a real princess at last, especially such a pretty one. They were married straightaway and lived a long and happy life together. And as for the three peas – they were put into the royal museum, where you can still see them today. That is, unless they have been stolen by someone who wants to find a real princess!

Pansy Pig

One squiggly, wriggly piglet can get into lots of trouble. Two squiggly, wriggly piglets are worse! Can you imagine what six squiggly, wriggly piglets might do? Poor Mrs Pig didn't have to imagine. From the moment her six piglets were born, they were trouble!

There was Percy, who just loved to stick his little pink snout into lots of things he should not.

There was Penny, who liked to explore . . . everything!

There was little Pickle, who was always getting lost.

There were Poppy and Pippa, the terrible two, who tried to eat the strangest things.

And there was Pansy, who got into more trouble than the other five piglets put together.

Now Pansy wasn't naughtier than Percy. She wasn't sillier than Poppy and Pippa. She certainly wasn't as brave as Penny and Pickle. So why did Mrs Pig have to give Pansy a "serious talk" at least three times a day?

Well, the other little pigs were as alike as five peas in a pod. They were squiggly and wriggly and wiggly and pink. They were pink all over from their twisty tails to their sniffly snouts. It was very, very hard to tell the five piglets apart.

Pansy was different. She was pink, too, but on her little pink bottom she had a brown splodge. It looked just like a pansy flower!

When Mrs Pig saw four little pink bottoms sticking out of the horse trough, munching something they shouldn't, she couldn't be sure who three of them were. But one little bottom had a beautiful brown pansy on it.

"PANSY!" yelled Mrs Pig. "Come out of that trough right now! And you too . . . er . . . you other three!"

It was the same when Mrs Pig saw five little piglets diving in the duck pond, upsetting the dabbling ducklings. Four of the piglets looked just the same. But one little piglet, who was splashily practising the piggy paddle, had a very familiar flower on her bottom.

49

"PANSY!" screeched Mrs Pig. "Come out of that pond right now! And you too . . . er . . . you other four!"

The ducks, the horses and the hens got used to hearing Mrs Pig shouting at all hours of the day and night.

"Pansy! PANSY! P-A-N-S-Y!"
The other squiggly piglets got used to it too. But Pansy didn't. It wasn't fair that she always got the blame . . . just because she was different.

Then, one drippy, droppy, drizzly day, all six little pigs got tired of staying in their pigsty and looking out at the rain.

"I'm going to explore!" squeaked Penny. She trotted out into the rain.

"Wait for me!" cried Pickle, scrambling after her.

"Can you eat rain?" squealed Poppy and Pippa, and scampered off to see.

"Let's splash in the puddles!" squeaked Percy, dashing out of doors.

And Pansy Pig, who didn't want to be left behind, rushed after him.

For the rest of the morning, six wet and wiggly piglets had a wonderful time. When they found that the bank of the pond was one big muddy playground, they couldn't believe their luck.

"Whee!" they skidded and slipped.

"Whoo!" they splished and sploshed.

"Whaa!" they rolled and wriggled.

When Mrs Pig came looking for six naughty little pink pigs, she couldn't find them at all. But she did see six dirty brown piglets covered in mud.

51

Mrs Pig opened her mouth to yell . . . and then shut it again. She couldn't be sure. Were these really her piglets? She looked for Pansy's familiar little bottom, but all she saw was mud, mud and more mud.

Mrs Pig tried to feel cross. But even when a big splodge of mud came flying across and hit her on the

ear, she couldn't manage it. She started to laugh. And the next minute, she couldn't resist it any longer. She jumped with a splat right into the mud and squiggled and wriggled herself.

"I love getting muddy!" squealed Pansy Pig.

"So do I" laughed Mrs Pig!

And a squiggly wriggly little piglet, who hadn't been shouted at all day, gave her big muddy mum a big muddy hug.

The Wheels on the Bus

The wheels on the bus go round and round,
Round and round,
Round and round,
The wheels on the bus go round and round,
All day long.

The horn on the bus goes beep beep beep,
Beep beep beep,
Beep beep beep,
The horn on the bus goes beep beep beep,
All day long.

The lights on the bus go blink blink blink,
Blink blink blink,
Blink blink blink,
The lights on the bus go blink blink blink,
All day long.

The doors on the bus, they open and shut,
Open and shut,
Open and shut,
The doors on the bus, they open and shut,
All day long.

The children on the bus go up and down,
Up and down,
Up and down,
The children on the bus go up and down,
All day long.

Aunty Octopus

Aunty Octopus is very kind. Whenever the baby sea creatures are upset they visit Aunty Octopus for a cuddle. She has so many arms that she can hug lots of them at the same time.

"I've lost my best shell," sobs Clownfish.

"Don't cry," says Aunty Octopus. "I'll find another one for you."

Aunty Octopus scoops up a pretty pink shell from inside her cave and throws it

to Clownfish. He pushes it along with his nose, laughing and wriggling his fins.

"Thank you!" cries Clownfish as he shoots away. Little Cora Crab is unhappy. "I do not feel well," she says. "My claws itch and my shell feels too tight."

"Do not worry," says Aunty Octopus. "You are about to grow a new shell. In a few days' time you will feel fine."

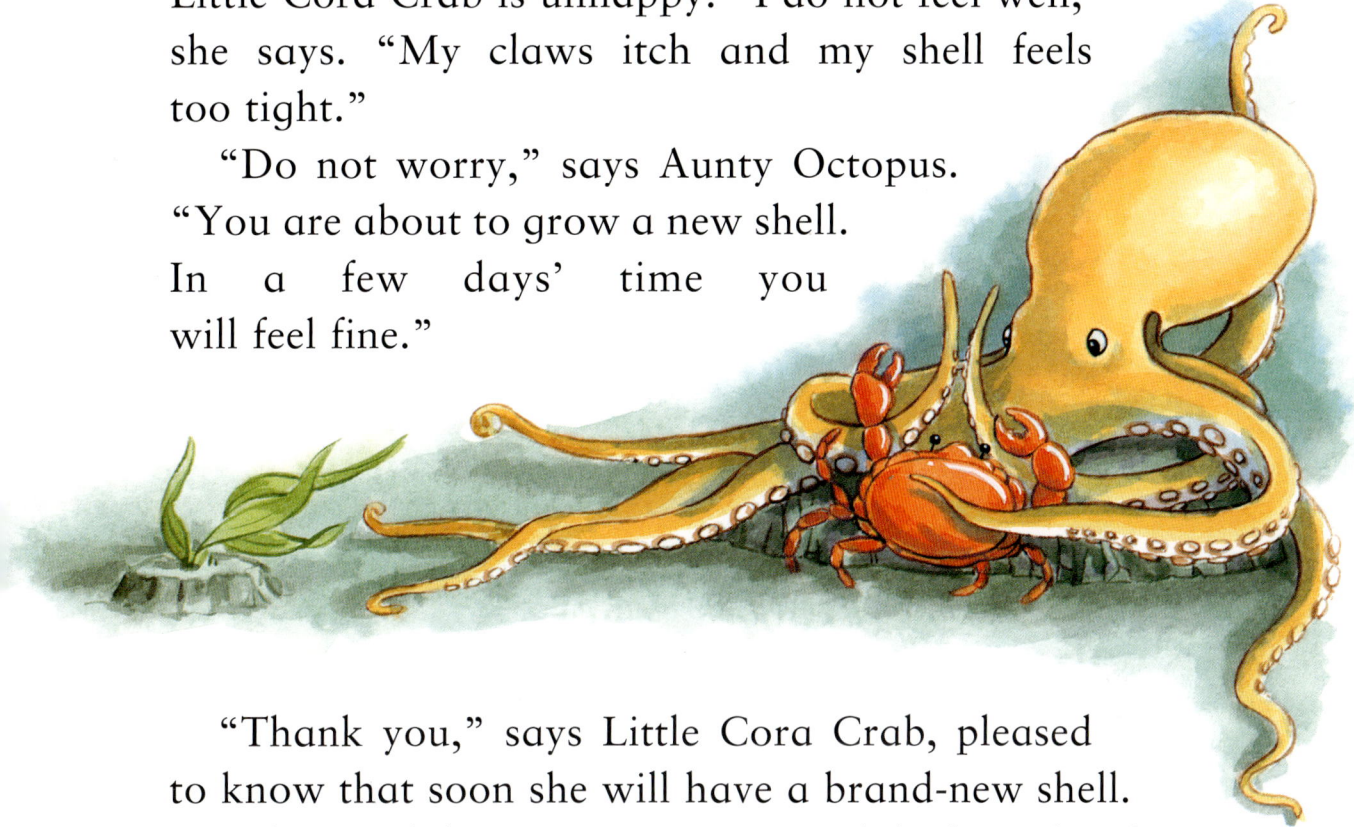

"Thank you," says Little Cora Crab, pleased to know that soon she will have a brand-new shell.

Baby Starfish is crying. Big tears slide down her face and drip off her points.

"I am lost!" she sobs. "I cannot find my way home."

"No problem!" says Aunty Octopus, mopping up the tears with a soft seaweed handkerchief. "I know where you live. Shall I take you back now?"

So off they go. Aunty Octopus carries the little starfish safely home in her big, gentle arms.

One day, Dippy Dolphin comes along to ask if Aunty Octopus can help him with his homework. Silky Seal arrives to tell her about a fight with his brother. And Timothy Turtle is feeling lonely and wants a hug.

"Aunty Octopus! Are you there?" calls Dippy Dolphin.

"Aunty Octopus! Where are you?" cries Silky Seal.

"Please come out and see us!" calls Timothy Turtle.

The little sea friends search everywhere but Aunty Octopus is nowhere to be found. Her cave is empty.

All at once, Wise Old Walrus comes diving down, shaking his whiskers.

"Whatever is the matter?" he asks.

"Aunty Octopus seems to have disappeared," explains Dippy Dolphin.

"Aha! Aha!" says Wise Old Walrus. "I saw Aunty swimming towards the wreck. She should be back by now, though."

"Perhaps poor Aunty is in trouble and needs our help," cries Timothy Turtle.

They all set off towards the wreck.

As they are skimming along, Nipper Shark swims up to join them.

"Go away! You might eat us," squeak Silky Seal and Dippy Dolphin. "Go away!"

"But I only want to help," calls Nipper Shark. "Aunty Octopus is my friend too, you know."

He swims along behind the others. When they reach the wreck they spot Aunty Octopus caught in an old fishing net. The

more she wriggles and tries to pull free, the more her eight arms get into knots.

"Thank heavens you have found me," she calls.

Timothy Turtle tries to undo the knots but soon his flippers are tangled.

Dippy Dolphin thrashes his tail at the net but his fins become caught too.

Silky Seal batters the net but is soon wound up into the knots.

"Stop it at once!" shouts Wise Old Walrus. "There is one young fellow here who can sort everything out. Come along, young Nipper Shark."

Nipper Shark swims up shyly. Then he bites a huge hole in the net. Aunty Octopus is set free. Now Nipper's rows of sharp teeth slice into the horrid net again and he frees the others too.

Aunty Octopus explains:

"I had gone to look for a present to cheer up Nipper Shark," says Aunty Octopus. "You are rather horrid to him, you know."

"We are frightened of your big sharp teeth," explains Silky Seal to the friendly little shark. "But now your sharp teeth have been very useful!"

"Without you, we should have been stuck in the net for ever!" add Dippy Dolphin and Timothy Turtle.

Now the friends are pleased to play games with Nipper Shark. They realize that he would never ever dream of eating a playmate! So they all play together happily every day as Aunty Octopus waves to them from her cave.

One, Two, Three, Four, Five

One, two, three, four, five,
Once I caught a fish alive.
Six, seven, eight, nine, ten,
Then I let it go again.
Why did you let it go?
Because it bit my finger so.
Which finger did it bite?
This little finger on the right.

Cluck, Cluck, Cluck

Cluck, cluck, cluck, cluck, cluck,
Good morning, Mrs Hen.
How many chickens have you got?
Madam, I've got ten.

Four of them are yellow,
And four of them are brown.
And two of them are speckled red,
The nicest in the town.

Thumbelina

O nce upon a time, there was a woman who wanted to have a child of her own. The years passed by and no child came. One day the woman went to see a witch. The witch gave her a stem of barley and told the woman to plant it in a flowerpot.

The woman did as she was told, and a beautiful flower grew. The petals of the flower were shut tight, so the woman kissed them. At once, the petals sprang open and the woman saw a tiny baby girl inside. The little girl was beautiful, but she was even tinier than the woman's

thumb. The woman and her husband decided to call her Thumbelina.

They gave the baby a walnut shell for a bed and a rose leaf for a blanket. She slept in the bed at night and played on the table during the daytime.

Then, one night, an ugly toad jumped onto the table where Thumbelina slept.

"RIBBET!"

"RIBBET!" croaked the toad. "She would make a perfect wife for my son." The toad grabbed Thumbelina as she slept and carried her away to her muddy home.

"RIBBET! RIBBET!" croaked her ugly son,

65

when he saw the beautiful Thumbelina.

"EEEK," screamed Thumbelina, when she saw the two ugly toads. "Ahhh!" she wailed, when the mother toad explained that she wanted Thumbelina to marry her ugly son.

The toads were afraid that Thumbelina might run away. They took her to a lily pad on the river. There was no way that Thumbelina could escape. She cried and she cried. When they heard her sobs, the little fish poked their heads out of the water. Charmed by her beauty, they decided to help the tiny girl. They chewed away at the stem that held the lily pad in place, until at last it was free. Thumbelina floated away.

She floated on and on down the river. Then, one day,

the wind blew so hard that Thumbelina was swept up into the air and carried onto the land.

All through the summer, Thumbelina lived alone in a big wood. However, when the winter came she soon felt hungry. She left the wood and made her way into a field. Before too long, she came to a door and knocked on it. When it was opened by a field mouse, Thumbelina begged her for something to eat. Luckily, the field mouse was a kind creature and she invited Thumbelina into her warm home. The field mouse soon grew to like Thumbelina and invited her to stay.

After Thumbelina had been there for a short time, the field mouse told her about her neighbour, Mr Mole.

"He's a very rich man. It would be wonderful if you could marry him. Of course, he is blind, so you will have to please him with your pretty voice."

But after meeting Mr Mole, Thumbelina did not

want to marry him at all. He was indeed rich, but he hated the sunlight and the flowers although he had never seen them. Mr Mole fell in love as soon as he heard Thumbelina's sweet voice. The field mouse and Mr Mole agreed that he would marry Thumbelina.

Mr Mole dug a tunnel between their two houses, and one day he gave Thumbelina a guided tour.

Halfway along the tunnel, Mr Mole kicked aside a dead bird.

"Stupid thing," he grumbled. "It must have died at the beginning of the winter." Thumbelina felt sorry for the bird, but she said nothing.

Later, when the field mouse was asleep, Thumbelina

crept back into the tunnel. "Good-bye, dear bird," she whispered. She pressed her head against the bird's chest and, to her surprise, she felt something move. The bird was not dead. It had lain asleep all winter and was now waking up

For the rest of the winter, Thumbelina nursed the bird and soon he was well. When spring arrived, Thumbelina smuggled him in through the tunnel and out of the field mouse's door.

"Good-bye," wept Thumbelina, as the bird flew away.

Time passed quickly, and soon Thumbelina's wedding day arrived. Wishing to get one last look at the outside world before entering Mr Mole's gloomy home, she walked in the field.

"Quiveet, quiveet," came a noise above her head. It was Thumbelina's bird friend. Seeing how unhappy the little girl was, he said, "I'm flying somewhere warm for the winter. Come with me. You can sit on my back."

Thumbelina quickly agreed and before too long she found herself in a wonderful warm place. The bird put Thumbelina down on the petals of a beautiful flower. To Thumbelina's surprise, a tiny man with wings was sitting in the centre of the flower. He was a flower fairy. Straightaway he fell in love with the tiny Thumbelina and asked her to marry him. Thumbelina happily agreed.

On their wedding day, Thumbelina received all kinds of presents. The best one of all was a pair of tiny wings. She used them to fly from flower to flower. At last Thumbelina was the happiest girl alive!

Jungle, Jungle!

Jungle, jungle! Sounds of the jungle!
"Squawk! Squawk!" Who is that?
A rainbow-striped bird with shiny feathers covering her back, and long sleek tail feathers stretching down. Her beak is hooked, top and bottom, and her eye is beady.

"Squawk! Squawk! I'm a macaw," says Macaw proudly.

Jungle, jungle! Sounds of the jungle.
"Croak! Croak!" Who is that?
A slippy slimy amphibian with a leathery skin, and large staring eyes that move about. Her toes are terribly sticky and help her to climb.

"Croak! Croak! I'm a tree-frog," croaks Tree-frog proudly.

Jungle, jungle! Sounds of the jungle.
   "O-o! O-o!" Who is that?
A big, wide-eyed mammal with long orangey hair. She likes chewing leaves and fruit, and spends most of her life swinging through the trees.

"O-o! O-o! I'm an orang-utan," says Orang-utan proudly.

Jungle, jungle! Sounds of the jungle.
   "Hi-ss! Hi-sssss!" Who is that?
A long-bodied reptile with a scaly skin, who twists and turns on the forest floor, slithering and sliding. His eyes are keen, and he flicks out his forked tongue.

"Hi-ss! Hi-sssss! I'm a swamp-snake," hisses Swamp-snake proudly.

Jungle, jungle! Sounds of the jungle.
   "Squelch! Squelch!" Who is that?
A dangerous mammal with not much hair. A creeping, frightening beast. Squelch! Squelch! Who could it be?

"Hide! Hide! Everyone hide," calls Snake.

"Wait!" calls Orang-utan. "Who could it be? Let's wait and see."

"Wait to be snapped by the jaws of a croc?" squawks Macaw.

"Wait to be torn by a leopard's sharp teeth?" croaks Tree-frog.

"Wait, wait!" replies Orang-utan. "I really want to know who it is – don't you?"

So they wait and see a two-legged, two-armed mammal, standing up and dressed in green. His two bright eyes are beady, aware. They are looking all around him, looking for someone, but who could it be?

"O-o, OK," whispers Orang-utan. "Let's hide everyone – O-o! NOW!"

Macaw hides high in the canopy of leaves. Tree-frog hides low on a waxy leaf. Snake curls his body by the swamp. And Orang-utan swings away, up, up into the tree, as fast as her strong arms can carry her.

Squelch! Hunter's footsteps. Squelch! Very near!
"Big breath everyone. All together now!"

Squawk! Squawk! Squawk! Croak! Croak! Hiss! Hissssss! Hiss!

"Help me! Help!" calls the frightened hunter.

Orang-utan sees the hunter running, and calls out loudly to her friends: "Big breath . . . everyone . . . all together now!"

"Squawk! O-o! Croak! Hiss! Squawk! O-o! Croak! Hiss!" scream all the animals.

The squelching footsteps go squelch, squelch, squelch ever so quickly the opposite way. And after the silence come the other sounds, the sounds of the jungle.

**Jungle, jungle! Sounds of the jungle.
Squawk! O-o! Croak! Hi-ss! Ha! Ha! Ha!**

75

Sing a Song of Sixpence

Sing a song of sixpence,
A pocket full of rye;
Four and twenty blackbirds,
Baked in a pie.

When the pie was opened,
The birds began to sing;
Wasn't that a dainty dish,
To set before the king?

The king was in his counting-house,
Counting out his money;
The queen was in the parlour,
Eating bread and honey.

The maid was in the garden,
Hanging out the clothes,
When down came a blackbird
And pecked off her nose.

Jack and Jill

Jack and Jill
Went up the hill,
To fetch a pail of water;
Jack fell down,
And broke his crown,
And Jill came tumbling after.

Then up Jack got,
And home did trot,
As fast as he could caper;
He went to bed,
To mend his head,
With vinegar and
brown paper.

Roly and Poly

Roly and Poly are polar bears. They live in the cold, frozen north where the wind blows and the snow snows. Roly and Poly like to play in the ice and the snow. They run and throw snowballs. They slide and skate. They play chasing games all day. They roll down the snowy slopes. They laugh and tumble. They ride on the icebergs. They swim

in the navy-blue sea. They are very, very happy little bears.

"Listen to me!" cries Roly, playing a tune by hitting a row of icicles with a stick.

"Now listen to me!" cries Poly, shouting "Hello! Hello!" in a loud voice into an echoing cave. The echoing cave shouts "Hello!" back at him.

"Listen to us!" shout Roly and Poly together, as their voices boom out a really loud, Big Bear song. They stamp out a merry dance together – moving round and round in circles over the snow.

"This is fun!" laughs Roly.

"This is great!" laughs Poly.

"Watch me!" shouts Roly, jumping to catch the biggest snowflakes you have ever seen.

"Watch me!" shouts Poly, leaping across a gap in the ice.

"Watch us!" shout Roly and Poly together, laughing as they slide all the way down from the Icy Ridge to the Deep Green Pool.

Splash! Splash! The two little bears tumble into the

freezing water.

"This is fun!" laughs Roly.

"This is great!" laughs Poly.

The bears' fur coats are soft and deep and cosy. They can stay warm all day, no matter how much the wind blows and the snow snows.

The air fills with their steamy breath as the bears climb out of the water and run down to the sea.

"I am tired now!" says Roly.

"So am I," says Poly.

"Let's sit down for a rest!" says Roly.

"What a good idea," says Poly.

The two bears look around them.

"That big grey rock looks a brilliant place to sit!" says Roly, pointing to a shape sticking out of the sea.

"Ooh, yes," says Poly. "It is nice and smooth."

Roly and Poly jump onto the big, smooth, grey rock and settle down for a rest before they begin playing their games again.

"This is a good rock!" says Poly.

"It's a great rock!" laughs Roly.

"I don't remember seeing it here before!" says Poly.

"No!" says Roly, "It must be a new one."

"I really am feeling very sleepy now!" says Roly.

"So am I," says Poly.

The two bears yawn and stretch, and then sit back to back. They lean against each other. They watch the lapping waves below.

First Roly's eyes start to close. Then Poly's eyes slide

shut. In no time at all both the bears are fast asleep.
The sky grows dark. The stars begin to twinkle. The
Moon rises, big and silvery.

All of a sudden, the grey rock starts to move. It slips
out into the cold sea. It moves past the icebergs and
through the waves. It bobs along, following
the path of the Moon.

In fact, the grey rock is not a
grey rock at all.

It is a humpback whale.
She has just woken up and decided to go for
a swim. She has no idea that two little bears are fast
asleep on her back. The whale decides to dive down.
The icy-cold water rushes up around her.

"Yeow!" yells Roly, waking up in the sea.

"Yeow!" yells Poly as waves splash onto his face.

The two bears are floating in the dark water – and they're a long way from home.

"Yeow!" they both call out together. "Yeow!"

Whale hears the bears' loud cries and comes back up to the surface.

"What are you two bears doing out here in the night?" she asks.

"I don't know!" says Roly.

"I don't know!" says Poly.

"We don't know!" say Roly and Poly together, and they start to cry.

"Well, I'd better take you home," says Whale. The two bears climb up onto her back.

"Your back looks very like the grey rock that we sat on," says Roly.

"I think your back *is* the grey rock that we sat on," says Poly.

Once they have realized that they will soon be safe, Roly and Poly enjoy their moonlight ride.

"This is fun!" laughs Roly.

"This is great!" laughs Poly.

"Thank you!" say Roly and Poly together.

Before long they are home again. Mother Bear is delighted to see her little bears are safe. She gives Whale a real polar bear hug and a big red shawl. Whale swims off, waving goodbye with her huge tail.

"Goodbye!" says Roly.

"Goodbye!" says Poly.

"Goodnight!" say Roly and Poly together.

The Gingerbread Man

Once upon a time there lived a little old man and a little old woman. The little old man and the little old woman were very happy except for one thing – they had no children. So, one day they decided to make a child for themselves. They rolled his body out of gingerbread, and used raisins for his eyes and nose, and orange peel for his mouth. Then they put him in the oven to bake.

When the Gingerbread Man was cooked, the little old woman opened the door and . . .

out jumped the Gingerbread Man and away he ran.

"Come back! Come back!" cried the little old man and the little old woman, running after him as fast as they could. But the Gingerbread Man just laughed, and shouted,

"Run, run as fast as you can. You can't catch me, I'm the Gingerbread Man!"

The little old man and the little old woman could not catch him, and soon they gave up. The Gingerbread Man ran on and on, until he met a cow.

"Moo," said the cow. "Stop! I would like to eat you."

"Ha!" said the Gingerbread Man. "I have run away

from a little old man and a little old woman, and now I will run away from you."

The cow began to chase the Gingerbread Man across the field, but the Gingerbread Man simply ran faster, and sang,

"Run, run, as fast as you can. You can't catch me, I'm the Gingerbread Man!"

The cow could not catch him. The Gingerbread Man ran on, until he met a horse.

"Neigh," said the horse. "Stop! I would like to eat you."

"Ha!" said the Gingerbread Man. "I have run away from a little old man, a little old woman and a cow, and now I will run away from you."

Then the horse began to chase the Gingerbread Man, but the Gingerbread Man ran faster and faster, and as he ran he sang,

"Run, run as fast as you can. You can't catch me, I'm the Gingerbread Man!"

The horse could not catch him, so the Gingerbread Man ran on, until he came to a playground full of children.

"Hey, Gingerbread Man," called the children. "Stop! We would like to eat you."

"Ha!" said the Gingerbread Man. "I have run away from a little old man, a little old woman, a cow and a horse, and now I will run away from you."

The children began to chase the Gingerbread Man but it was no good, the Gingerbread Man was just too quick for them.

While he ran he sang,

"Run, run as fast as you can.
You can't catch me,
I'm the Gingerbread Man!"

By now, the Gingerbread Man was feeling very pleased with himself. "No one will ever eat me," he thought, as he came to a river. "I am the cleverest person alive."

Just then, a fox appeared and came towards the Gingerbread Man.

"I have run away from a little old man, a little old woman, a cow, a horse and a playground full of children, and now I will run away from you," shouted the Gingerbread Man.

"Run, run, as fast as you can. You can't catch me, I'm the Gingerbread Man!"

"I don't want to eat you," laughed the fox. "I just want to help you cross the river. Why don't you jump onto my tail and I'll carry you across?"

"Okay," said the Gingerbread Man, and up he hopped. When the fox had swum a little way he turned to the Gingerbread Man and said, "My tail is getting tired. Won't you jump onto my back?"

So the Gingerbread Man did.

A little farther on, the fox said to the Gingerbread Man, "You are going to get wet on my back. Won't you jump onto my shoulder?"

So the Gingerbread Man did.

Then just a bit farther on, the fox said to the

Gingerbread Man, "Quickly, my shoulders are sinking. Jump onto my nose. That way you will keep dry."

So the Gingerbread Man did, and before he knew it the fox had flipped the Gingerbread Man up into the air and gulped him down in a single bite.

The poor Gingerbread Man wasn't so clever after all, was he?

Twinkle, Twinkle, Little Star

Twinkle, twinkle, little star,
How I wonder what you are,
Up above the world so high,
Like a diamond in the sky,
Twinkle, twinkle, little star,
How I wonder what you are.

Star Light, Star Bright

Star light, star bright,
First star I see tonight,
I wish I may, I wish I might,
Have the wish I wish tonight.

Hush-a-Bye, Baby

Hush-a-bye, baby,
On the treetops,
When the wind blows,
The cradle will rock.
When the bough breaks,
The cradle will fall,
Down will come baby,
Cradle and all.

93